The ENDLESS REPETITION
of an ORDINARY MIRACLE

The Endless Repetition of an Ordinary Miracle

Poems

Marjory Heath Wentworth

Press 53
Winston-Salem, NC

Press 53
PO Box 30314
Winston-Salem, NC 27130

First Edition

A TOM LOMBARDO POETRY SELECTION

Cover design by Kevin Watson

Cover art, "Abodes," copyright © 2010 Mary Edna Fraser

Author photo by Karen Ray Donner

Printed on acid-free paper

ISBN 978-0-9825760-6-9

For Ellie Maas Davis and Periel Llewellyn

Contents

Part III

Part IV

Acknowledgments

Grateful acknowledgement is made to the editors of the following publications in which these poems first appeared, some in slightly different versions:

Lady Jane's Miscellany, Issue 1 Summer 09: "Annunciation"

Nimrod International Journal, *Crossing Borders*, Spring/Summer 2007, Vol 50. No 2: "Nocturne 2006"

Charleston Magazine, Jan/Feb. 2009: "Perhaps an Angel Looks Like Everything We Have Forgotten"

The Dead Mule School of Southern Literature, Spring 2009: "Charleston Rooftops," "Pine Pitch," "Grief the Color of Dahlias," "The Geography of Home," "Nothing Can Contain You"

The Corltand Review, Issue 44 August 2009: "Spaghetti"

The Southern Women's Review, Issue I: "Stillborn"

South Carolina Poetry Initiative Chapbook Web Anthology (University of South Carolina): "Begin Again" and "Senility"

Sporting Words, Sports Poetry Anthology Trading Cards: "Skiing"

The author would like to thank the Spring Island Trust, Virginia Center for the Creative Arts, the Vermont Studio Center, and the Block Island Poetry Project where some of these poems were written. She would also like to thank editor Tom Lombardo and publisher Kevin Watson at Press 53, who care passionately about literature.

I

What If

the coin landed on heads instead of tails

wind blew in another direction

a boat landed here   the storm turned north

the car stopped before the patch of black ice

fire never spread through the house

the bomb never dropped   the bullet missed its mark

What if grass was worshipped and Bach prevailed

Bonhoeffer had succeeded   Europeans

had revered the Indians   angels were

visible   war was a memory

everyone forgot   what if the light

within us found a way to burn bright

Begin Again

Come through the doorway
without anger and your multitude of masks.
Look into the mirror on the wall
at the bottom of the stairs. Discover
desire, the way it felt before you came
here, before you smelled the sea.
Remove everything but
the future, where flowers are
strewn across a bed. No secrets.
Begin again. Tell me about
the courage to bloom, the way
wood shines in your house,
where you rise each day and plan
ways to fill the hours. It is like building
a boat of bruised days made from twisted hands.
Still, the molding garden buried in snow
reminds me of the suffering
you will not speak of, anywhere

Annunciation

For Harriet Popham Rigney

the Archangel is expected   almost
kneeling   robes flowing like water

against the late afternoon   silence
dominating   the room's internal

order   in the corner   Mary
paused in prayer   head down

hesitant   wrapped in blue wool
she sits beneath a dove   ringed by fire

such resistance in the air
not the room   as the pattern

is certain   long rectangled
windows   holding daylight

the floor   composed of diamonds
gray and brown   squares

red   white starred   red
dress   the bed draped in silk

square white pillow at rest
such stillness   at the center

of this story   *fleur de lys*
in bloom   the world outside

the window   diminished
as the room transforms into a kind

of reliquary   everything
sacred   swirling towards night

Geography of Home

Sudden winter rain   a need   like night
camellias that morning   startling

a thing remembered   how we fill
our days   of ornaments

unwrapped and scattered across
the kitchen table   chocolates

in a silver box from home   wind
white and furious   watching

the first hour of *Fanny and Alexander*
Christmas Eve   snow falling   candlelight

feast at the end of day   a family
gathered   and then, the stark unraveling

ice breaking on the river
beside the house   the children

shocked into submission
reality   broken ever since

That night   a voice on the phone
once held me   steady

sometimes that is enough   a man
with a full heart   and stories

thick snow on a lake   white breath
of horses   small children digging

tunnels in the fields beside the house,
afternoons with an English novel or the film,

because he misses home, but won't say
this is where he asked her

to marry him   under the stars
a bottle of champagne wedged

in a snowbank   as if songs were true
stories   as if joy could be anything but

elusive   promises made
before God   sometimes

a sudden turn in one direction
or another   eyes that meet

or do not   across the bar
the risked kiss   unbuckled belt

and so it goes   a stranger
came out of his house

to speak to a woman   this was
as calculated as a long voyage

shaving cream caught in his ear
this too was planned   one thing

on his mind   his stories as old as the sea—
the first stab to his heart

home on holiday leave   that night
     and the snow was falling

her hair was full of snow   or stars
caught on their eyelashes   and tears

he got down on his knees   his uniform
shining buttons   none of that mattered

he moved in   they wore
the same size jeans   they fit

like them   no arguing with that
forget the world   *let us*

be happy when we are happy
the story that stays with me—

his submarine surfacing
into a swarm of monarchs

crossing the Atlantic   mid day
no clouds   the wonder of it

so much sunlight   with you
it is something like that

he said   and then
a child conceived because

of me   the memory of   that
story not written anywhere

My Quaker Grandmothers

It is 1900, and my grandmother has arrived
in the middle of July like a new planet in the sky.

Firstborn and adored, she is dressed
in a long white cotton gown for the photograph.

While she sleeps, she curls her fist
around her mother Marion's index finger.

Marion, seated like a queen in a throne,
holds my grandmother's face toward the camera.

Married to a railroad Baron, my great grandmother
wants for nothing in the world. But she is Quaker,

and what she wants she already has. There are stories
about refusing jewels and elaborate gifts, no wine

in the home, only a bottle of whiskey for snake bites,
books overflowing in the library, a garden

of old English roses, rosemary, and mint growing
beside the sprawling house built purposely in the shade.

Marion's mother and grandmother stand stiffly
on either side of the chair. Their starched black dresses

cover everything but their grim faces. Hair tied back
into knots, heads covered in white bonnets—

no one is smiling on this joyous occasion.
The women look down toward my grandmother

the way all eyes look toward Christ
in certain nativity paintings. The ones

where angels bow their heads, and the infant
is the only one facing the heavens.

Atlantic City May 1904

The boardwalk bustles with people passing
back and forth between the grand hotels and the sea.

Everyone wears a hat, even my four-year-old grandmother.
Hers is wheat-colored straw and wide-brimmed.

It frames her face like a halo. A satin sky
blue ribbon tied into a bow at her right temple

keeps the blond curls from blowing across her forehead
in the wind that follows her everywhere.

She holds her favorite doll Dinah in front of her.
This doll, she kept in perfect condition

until the day she died, is stitched from thick black cotton.
With a red bandana wrapped around her head,

rows of bright necklaces clinging to her neck,
and a starched white apron tied around the waist,

Dinah is dressed like a Caribbean fruit seller.
She is half the size of my grandmother, and never

stops smiling. In the background, a black man
wearing a suit and a derby cap leans over the metal railing.

One foot placed in front of the other, the man in the photograph
seems poised to walk out onto the sea and never return.

And no one passing on the boardwalk seems to notice
or care about the one who is turning away.

Senility

Silent for hours, she   sat
at her window and   watched   wind
tearing at the dead   dried leaves,
until they   smothered the ground.
My grandmother   used to talk
non-stop. Fluent   in seven
languages, her favorite thing
was   singing   Christmas   carols
in   German all year long.   *Why wait*
all year for the holidays,
she wondered. *I could be gone*
by the Fourth of July!
She wasn't gone that summer,
but her mind   seemed to   be
slowly unraveling.   She
didn't   notice   when she went
into a world   where trees were
catching   fire   and flying
across the sky of her   room
filled with   odorless horses
refusing to eat   when trains
and steamships passed   in the halls.
Someone   kept   slashing her clothes
with a   machete. She claimed
there was   a Mexican man
hiding all day   in the closet
who only came out   at night.
Hell's Bells, that is what happens
when a woman is left on
her own, she'd say   with a grin.
According to her, the fetus

in my   belly   wasn't   a baby.
Babies come in   small parts.
I should   go   to the   hospital
to pick up   one   part   at a time.
The head was first,   of course.
It was the   size   of a baseball,
although when women give birth
it's usually   a litter
of   puppies, or   if she's lucky –
one full grown   black   cat that comes
already named something cute.
While she   talked, she sat up   straight
in her bed,   surrounded by
pink   blankets, chewing   the frayed
corner of the TV   changer
which she often   mistook for
a Hershey's   Chocolate   Bar.
I sat in a   chair beside
the   window and listened,
one hand   in hers, the other
holding   my swollen   belly,
watching   the leaves   falling.

Spaghetti

Aunt Barbara was a beauty queen. Competing in the Miss America Pageant
and riding on top of floats in holiday parades in South Paris, Maine
did nothing to prepare her for being a wife. When she was first married
to Uncle Buddy, she knew how to boil water and cook spaghetti,
but the sauce was simply too much for her. So, she mixed catsup
into a little hot water left at the bottom of the pot,
poured it over the pasta, tossed in a lot of Kraft Parmesan Cheese
and served it almost every night. Uncle Buddy ate bowlfuls
of the stuff for months and told her it was delicious.
When my grandfather told me this story, he said
it's the kind of thing that happens when you really fall in love.
It was a summer evening. He was sitting in the Adirondack
chair behind the driveway in front of the railroad tracks
that ran through the yard behind my grandparents' house.
He smoked his pipe and talked while I pulled rhubarb from the garden.
We were waiting for Uncle Buddy and Aunt Barbara
to come in for the weekend, with my teenage cousins
who had long straight black hair and jeans so tight they had to lie down
on the bed to zip them up. On Saturday night, they played 45s
out in the shed and danced with the local boys.
And if we hadn't bothered them too much during the day,
they would let me and my cousins watch them through the window
and dance to Elvis and the Beatles out on the grass,
my grandparents sitting back in their chairs watching us,
tapping their feet and clapping until the train roared through town.

Stillborn

Blue jays zigzag through leafless
black branches at the edge of
the winter field where a cow
has lain three straight days, since
birthing a stillborn calf.
When she moans, the cry comes from
the great gulf of grief that is
motherhood. One tree trembling,
alone, red berries on tips
of the tallest branches,
this is what the cow sees
through air, the color of tears.

II

What Shines

Tears falling that no one sees   familiar
voices   voices you love and the bells
ringing at the end of day   seedlings
sprouting on the windowsill   the future
fish scales   iced branches   after
the storm   a choir   cloud covered stars
everyone's soul   white candles glowing
at the church entrance   desire   unspent
coins in a saucer   hair filled with sunlight
or water   what the diamond means

Saturday Morning on Broad Street

Where flowers are never forgotten
behind walls of stone and all that has
gathered   coins and smoke
church bells like wind   just here
beneath a cloud clotted sky   the scent
of last night's rain   ladies
wearing cotton blouses   doing laundry
in the little white room downstairs
they say the funniest things   later
a wedding out on the lawn   voices at dusk
violins   tea olives   a cardinal
brightening the fig tree   my heart

The Comet

While frost whitens the windows and snow
sifts through the air, we drink
Vodka from the bottle and dance
to reggae until we sweat. We should
scrape ice from the glass and watch
the comet streaking across the sky,
but we are dancing in this warm room
lit by candles. There is so much
light swirling around us,
that we must close our eyes to see.

All Things are Palpable, None are Known

Like a cosmic buzz this
low pitched thrum, tuning
itself in the background
of every room I enter.
Unexpected, in the way
a smile can suddenly
spread across a stranger's face,
but familiar also as
a train passing in the distance. It is
night, and memories attach
themselves to that sound
and the piece of moonlight
trying to push through a sky
cluttered with clouds. I am not
dreaming. There is rain
chiming the tin roof. Familiar
things seem distant. A stranger
once touched my hair
because it looked like the sun
was trapped there. And that was all.
It doesn't matter where
this happened or how much light
was in the sky. I only remember
the words. After that, silence.

Into This Sea I Spill

clouds scattered like thought   the sound
the train makes   scars   that still pull
from within   words that matter
sleepless nights   childhood entire
all manner of birds   and what they have
seen   each forgotten
yet lingering dream   the skin
lining my heart   a small boat
filling   with winter   moonlight.

Trappings

Blame it on the sand   in my shoes
two days later and so many
thousands   of miles away or stones
gathered on that   empty   beach—
marbled yellow, earthbound, scarred
with   glitter   as if starlight
was caught   inside, or   the mystery
of   the shipwreck   off the bluff
and how we   imagine it, stuck
in darkness. Maybe it's the way
white stone walls   weave across the island
like vines, as if   the earth   composed them,
gulls always   hovering in the background,
the stream of   geese that woke me   each morning,
your voice   when you close your eyes and   sing.
Blame it on the sea   trapped in your heart.

Honey Moonlight Rain

Night pulls him toward her.
All day he tried
to enter the bright wind
where she exists.
It was like watching
a bird soar past
the window. Beyond
the bridge, the river
turns from white froth
into something dark
and still. He trembles
when his arms move
around her body—
part silk, part rock,
part rain. The river
holds the wind
between its teeth.
Up and down her
spine, his hands swirl
like two happy fish.
He lifts the hair
from her neck.
Gathering all of it
in his arms, he dives
into the tangle of honey,
moonlight, and rain.
He wants to drown.
He finds her mouth.
His fingers flow
across her shoulders

as if they could touch
every inch of skin
at the same time
in the same place,
as if he is entering
a body of water
he remembers.

Why I Run

November and still   honeysuckle blooms
along the slim   path to the pond. Palmettos
and pines compose   the sky, but the empty   space
beneath   the tangle of branches   is an infinite

accumulation   of dust and stillness,   adrift
in the   confusion   of seasons. A box turtle
makes   an imperceptible crossing   through layers
of needles   fallen like seconds   through the day—

the time   it takes   to slide from one
watery world into another,   hours passed
in reverie, a kind of   floating   minutes
of a day filled with   purpose   and peace.

Six white herons feeding   at the edge of the pond.
I don't know what   binds them   to one another,
but their   patience   is certain. They came from a place
where bells mark   the hour and nothing else

where time   exists   like a body of water
that stretches the reflection   of a single pine tree
from one shore to   another. And the ginkgoes
are   always   flaming at the water's edge.

Morgan's Farm, Indiana

The longer I run
through   mist   drifting
across paths   that wind

through Morgan's Farm
past cows   bellowing
at the fence   and hunt dogs

dashing back and forth
in their pens,   the closer
I am to   the horses

bowing   silently   in the fields
as if they   pray
and I am allowed to join.

Skiing

sliding   across the rim

of the world through   sun washed air

past snow   coated evergreens

woods   filled with swirling   prisms

of splintered light   caught in ice

endlessly multiplying

into   silence   that flows

suddenly inside   you

III

What Passes

The old man in a plaid pressed shirt

walking two Scotties around the traffic circle

pick-ups bursting with Mexican lawn workers

a Buddhist monk in Nikes and a baseball cap

clumps of housewives on cell phones   a stream

of white kids   wet hair in clumps pedaling home

from the pool   towels damp   clinging

to their necks like rigging holding them down

in the fume filled wind   trucks grinding

at the edges of the neighborhood   a swirl

of sulphur   butterflies   sirens in the distance

the tragedy of a stranger's life unfolding

a beaten wife with the phone in her hand

flattened carcasses of squirrels   unseen

alligators   a box turtle on its long trek to the pond

the shy widower watering roses in the dark

too many drunks behind the wheel   that loneliness

clouds wondering the sky like lost objects   or found

dreams of young boys on skateboards   complacency

never enough compassion or birdsong

Spring Island, South Carolina

beyond clusters of dark birds   hovering
at the edge of sky   the wind bends yellow
tipped marsh grass rippling around a rim
of sand   uninterrupted waves spilling
one on top of the other   as everything
spins into salt   into sunlight
houses rise like castles   built on sand
each home   an alchemy of conquest
fire   hope   for there is more
light than we can hold   the end always
flowing like water   what we become
in the diffusion of divinity   across
the blind distance   light emanates
from a flaming sky   this is the world
at war   the air is bright and blessed
but the land is bent by hands of fire   burning
where islands dream at the edge of sky

History

After Lowell

I Salem

Twice a year ships sailed from Shanghai
to Salem. Stacked in their hulls were sacks
of oranges and rice, tins of tea, saffron
in glass bottles and rows of twine bound carpets
more colorful than the Puritan imagination.
Centuries later, these carpets swirled
across the polished floors of Victorian houses
north of Boston. Summers at our grandparents
house near the sea, where we lived
whenever our parents' lives fell apart,
my brother and I pretended that the rust
colored border of the living room rug,
was the edge of a cliff we couldn't cross.
In high ceilinged rooms, where we played
quietly among the antiques, dust filled
velvet curtains draped the lead glass windows
facing Atlantic Avenue. Behind them
it was as dark and cool as a cave.

A broken grandfather clock stood
beside the front door. Light blue moons
smiled from the corners of the clock face.
Sometimes my father's retarded sister stood
in the corner across from the clock and stared
for hours until someone noticed she was there.
Time was her one obsession. In this family
filled with genius, her mind seemed stuck.
One evening my father stood on a step ladder
beside her. He decided to fix the clock,
which had never worked in my lifetime.

II Sullivan's Island

In our gate house near the sea,
the shutters hang uneven on their hinges,
and the wood frame windows are swollen shut.
My husband tried to open one,
and the glass shattered in his hands.
Someone sanded the tongue and groove walls
until the Civil War bullet holes faded
then disappeared, like the Africans who once lived here.

We fill the rooms with antiques from the north—
my grandparents' dining room furniture,
cedar sea chests, polished silver and an oriental carpet
older than the rotting wood that holds this house
improbably together. The carpet once lay upon
my grandparents' floor like an ocean spreading
in every direction. Ships that came here
carried human beings in their hulls, not spices,
rice, or woven wool. Now the sea
roars incessantly. Along the back fence,
trumpet vines are thriving where our sons
dig trenches for a Lego fort under siege.
Palmettos rise from the grass.
Stacks of fallen fronds surround the boys,
whose fort is filled with holes—wide
enough to let in dust, snakes, and sunlight.

Old Burial Hill

It is good to walk through old cemeteries
and count small white headstones
of the babies and mothers who died
giving birth, soldiers and fishermen
who fought the British, lying inches away.

It is good to rub your hands over
worn letters carved into gravestones,
consider the collective suffering
of these families, then listen
to the silence of stone. It is good

to go down to Red's Pond and feed
stale chunks of bread to the ducks,
then watch the old men race little wooden boats
on Sunday mornings and feel
as if my grandfather and father were still

standing on either side of me. Each one
holding my hands the way they would
in winter, when they guided me across
the frozen pond until I let go and skated
across the ice without them. It is good

to wander the curved narrow roads
of Old Marblehead, past crowded rows
of well-kept captains' homes
and street gardens filled with roses
draped across white wood fences.

At the bottom of the hill, vines weave
through frayed stacks of lobster pots
heaped high beside the fish houses
at Gas House Beach. A hundred years ago,
lobsters washed-up on the sand in piles,

pots overflowing and bursting.
My grandfather fed claws to chickens
and tossed the shells back to sea. At low tide
you can walk to the island on a thin trail
of slick rocks, worn glass, feathers, and blue—

black mussel shells, watch the boats set sail—
gulls gathered on the rigging like snow.
The low groan of the horn is the sound
of my childhood. As I walk the rim
of the harbor, fog trails the edges of morning.

The air is tinged with gasoline, salt, fish.
Like a lid slid over the harbor,
the uninterrupted slate sky
is the color of graves and winter sea.
There is nothing easy about this history.

But it is good to remember where you come from.
At the top of Fort Sewall I face Children's Island.
Seagulls skim the rocks. Someone is playing
bagpipe music across the Sunday morning stillness
My father is trying to tell me something.

Charleston Rooftops

Everything that lifts into the air
has purpose: even the granite tipped war
monument rising above palmetto trees
points like an arrow toward the sun;
chimneys, stove pipes, weather vanes and steeples—
the flag at half mast, flapping in the wind.

Streets clog with memories of smoke tinged wind—
of a dark sky on fire fueling the air,
flames swirling around steeples,
and a harbor blocked by ships of war.
Cannons fired toward the ever present sun
until the avenues lined with oak trees

were abandoned, and the trees
thrust transcendent into the wind
reached like prayers toward the sun.
Odors of ruin and rot lingered in the air
above the streets emptied by war,
the bells silent in the steeples.

Beyond scaffold enshrouded steeples,
sunlight weaves through leaf-thick oak trees
now filled with blossom and song, though war
saturates the brick and memory of wind
spinning with salt through summer air
that simmers beneath the blood streaked sun.

Red runs through ribbons of sun
across the skyline and steeples
lifting off tin sloped roofs into air
filled with flowering trees.
Always the tireless ocean wind
ripples the worn-out flags of war.

The names of the enemy change, but war
is the inscrutable language spoken beneath this sun.
The flag at half-mast stiffens in the wind.
Funeral bells sound from the steeples.
In the cemetery, beneath the oak trees,
taps linger on the broken air.

The sounds of war will rumble in the wind.
As steeple bells call through the sun filled air,
birds nest in trees twisting toward heaven.

Elysium, Islands of the Blessed

Spring Island, South Carolina

In a building built   on sand
beneath a   blurry dome
of heaven, where islands   dream

beyond   bones and smoke
of a shattered   war, where the air
is bright and   blessed, I sleep

because there is   no sound
like   rain. I sleep
with windows   open   to wind

swirling through   pines and all
that is   carried with the sea.
Parris Island's hourly   splatter—

artillery practice,   day and night,
low flying plane roaring   overhead
in choreographed   circles,

where the dead   and the living
flow together,   I sleep
and dream   of war. 1951

my   teenage father
running laps   for hours
in the rain. Mud filled   shoes,

mouthfuls   of blood and salt.
At dawn and   in the dark
with a blindfold   and a broken toe,

tin roofs blurring   like oceans
at the edge of   his vision, as if
he is already   at sea   running

laps   around the flight deck,
as if he is already   a warrior as far
away   from home   as he can be.

the young pilot   circling
at the   edge   of the sky
veers back, follows the   curve

of a slow   thick river. Descending
through fists   of wind
filled rain. He   remembers

where he is going, sees the map
of the ancient   world creased
and taped above   his mother's stove,

palm trees and   fig leaves
sketched   around the yellowed edge,
Tigris and Euphrates   joined

flowing straight   into the sea.
Rivers   carrying Eden
carrying him   into the violent

uncertainty, waters   passing
Babylon,   where the gates of God
are opening   like lilies

I awaken   to the roar
of the plane   the sound
of terror   rippling

across time and the whole
world   ripening   rotting.

Nocturne 2006

1
Owls call from the hollows.
This is the sound of the moon.

Light shattering like glass
across the night. Sky

filled with ghosts. They have
traveled far. This room holds

their voices like a box
of cracked bones. I remember

how to write my name
in a swirl of Arabic.

It is a secret. Sound,
like the sound of my name

in the halls where I walked
through moonlight, stepping

over soldiers facing Mecca.
The faces of the tortured are

familiar. Beneath hoods, a voice
I recognize. A muscled thigh, feet

in shackles, buttocks and kneecaps.
Skin smelling of sweat and urine.

2.
A man is named for a prophet.
He calls for him in the darkness.

Naked and cold in a cage,
his middle name is God.

Schindlerjuden

This is a day with ghosts in it
Carol Ann Davis, "Winter Mix"

Stopped outside the walls of the Old City
men in suits, women in their best dresses
flapping in the wind, hand in hand
wings tucked. Sudden silence at the Gate.

Through the cool darkened passage
which feels like a cave, they enter
in pairs, like walking backwards
into the memory of what binds them.

As if doves composed of ash
were poured from the mouth
of the heart's bell—they emerge
in a multitude of clear voices singing.

It is midday and the air is thick and still
in the Catholic Cemetery when they climb
into the blinding Jerusalem sunlight
after passing beneath the shadow

of a cross. Slipping into a steady stream
of survivors and descendants, they move
slowly and deliberately to place a stone
on the grave of their savior. And the sky

is filled with the hum of the righteous
where there are no walls
or maps, just bones dissolving
in wind, and the history of stones.

Kambujan Eulogy

Cambodia, 1980

Above the graves at Tonle Sap
pagodas crumble and blend into earth.
Water drips from the bronze genie of the sky.
Four faces stare from the shadows:
eight arms, each one holding carved moons,
birds, children. A chipped sun
in the palm of the highest upturned palm
pushes through curling ferns like an offering.

This is where the monks return to pray.

Boat People

In Geneva, where everything's labeled
in five languages, words take on imagined
meanings. In 1979, Pol Pot seemed
like a misspelled name for a cooking dish,
and the news from Asia was getting tiresome.
In this tidy city built at the edge
of a lake, stories surfaced in a continuous
stream. After days of listening
to starved, scarred Cambodian refugees
describe the genocide they barely survived,
I rode on the back of a motorcycle
to Montreux where Herbie Hancock and Chick Corea
were playing duets on a red oriental carpet.
On stage, in the swirl of spot lights and smoke,
their pianos faced each other. At first
they seemed like boxers in a ring, then more
like lovers, laughing through the charged air passing
between them. After a while the music
was like a fruit split in half in my mouth,
the sharp and flat of one note becoming whole
within me. I listened, with my stoned Swiss friends,
until I forgot the cruel cacophony of stories
I wish I had never heard. That morning
a lice covered boy described how soldiers
sliced his mother's breasts off with an ax.
She was going to have a baby he said
between bites of a chocolate bar.
*She was tired all the time and couldn't
work quickly enough* . His voice was soft
and steady. As he spoke, he watched swans
gliding across the lake outside the office window.

That night, Herbie Hancock was smiling
like he had never known such horror,
but it must be the opposite—
all that joy tumbling out of sorrow.

In Gaza's Berry Fields

Layers of clouds have cooled the air
until the paths beside rows of strawberry plants
are filled with families. Children run
around the edge of the field, tossing handfuls
of berries into white plastic buckets and each other—
hands and mouths stained pink with juice.

A woman straightens up to rest her back.
She looks for her sons who helped
all morning. They're playing marbles
with their friends near the roadside,
tracing circles in the dirt with a sharp stick,
taking aim and shooting fast. Their laughter
floats through the sky until it reaches her.

Something hot passes over her head. It feels
like her hair is on fire, but she knows the sound
of mortars and the smell that follows.
Before she has time to run and grab her sons, a shell
explodes in the middle of the berry field. The sky
fills with smoke and a brief hard silence.

A tank rolls past. Shredded bodies are scattered
across the strawberry fields. The soldiers gather parts
into piles near the road, where the boys were
playing marbles. The mother runs, tearing at
her white head scarf, as she moves through the path
in the middle of the berry field. The head
of her youngest son is on the greenhouse roof.

She pulls it down, kisses it, puts it in her lap,
and wraps it in her scarf. A hand is caught
in a tree above the greenhouse. She grabs it,
kisses the fingers, places the hand beside the head,
ties the ends of the white cloth into a tight knot
and holds the bundle to her breast. Blood begins

to spread across the fabric. Her middle son's torso
lies in the dirt near the piles of body parts. Legs
are lined up beside it. She picks up a small leg
with a sandal still attached. Wiping away the blood,
she kisses the toes and puts the foot in the bundle
she will hold against her body forever.

She sits down against the wall and tries to lift
her arms toward heaven. Her hands are chopping
the smoke in front of her, as if they can show
how her children were torn apart, or how
her heart feels. When a soldier walks by,
she grabs the end of his rifle and points it

at her belly. The soldier is young,
but older than her sons, who were just
playing marbles at the edge of a field
on a winter morning in January in Northern Gaza,
while their mother filled the last bucket of the day
with sweet, ripe strawberries.

IV

What Remains

white feathers   in the nest   like a dusting of snow
emptiness of birth   after prayers   paint drying
on the canvas   it is raining   blue egg
in a glass   Jim Crow   hidden in their hearts
a city divided   scars   in every home   the Gospel
truth   at the bottom of an empty puddle   silence
when the last breath is taken   days scratched
on the prison wall   shreds of silk   and sunlight
lining the abandoned   chrysalis   after the storm
the broken house   floating like a boat   a voice
filled with bells   bed of leaves   ashes
on the mantle   history is the container
buried beneath the killing fields   a white string
still tied to a baby's wrist   and bones   clinging
together   across the miles   in the hotel of stars
iron and straw   a field of winter   fields of milk
the permanence of snow   and the arithmetic
after childhood   that sack of small stones
we carry   a heart filled with scars   the sea
holding too many bones   despite genocide
so many creatures in the air   fluttering
over the graves   and the onion domes
inside   memories of what is found there

What the Shrine Wants

Beneath prayer flags strung across the top
of the windowpane, beside the arc
of baleen shredding in the corner
balanced against a red candle squeezed
into a glass stickered with blue-eyed Santa Barbara
holding a chalice in one hand, sword
in the other, who is, according to the text painted
along the side—*a sublime and generous
protector*—on the white shelf
where the Buddhist shrine holds
photographs of the departed, prayer cards,
funeral programs, feathers and stones;
a small brown bird leaps like a fish
against the window. Over and over
in the light that hovers around this cluster
of souls, a small bird keeps rising
until he rests among the sweet faces,
the bleached shark vertebrae, birch bark,
sage bound in blue string and one stone
rubbed smooth in an earthquake.

Perhaps an Angel Looks Like Everything We Have Forgotten

Picture the stars that wait in silence
while you remember songbirds
calling behind closed curtains
of a bedroom window, and the soft hum
of cicadas permeating the walls of a dream,
because you let them. When you were small
you gave yourself time to imagine
everything beyond the glass,
while you waited for night to unravel,
holding onto pieces as long as you could.
Wood smoke carried across the orchard,
a willow tree you passed on the way to school,
the smell of wet leaves underfoot,
but this time you were flying above the trees
with your cousin who drowned the summer
before. Hovering like kites over the town,
it felt like you were being pulled, as if someone
held strings that tugged and gave you direction.
Had you ever felt safer or happier?

What is left of that body composed
of stardust and flame? Little bones
buried at the bottom of the sea,
where it is dark and still, and that is why
night becomes the place for grief.

But the night is long and you imagine
where the wind has been and what you have
lost. On St. Simons island, where freed slaves
built towns as if hope flowed
in the rivers running through,

you face foghorns and the roar of the sea,
the wind like someone's heart beating
against you. If the sea could
teach one thing, it would be acceptance.
Why live all this time, if not to love
the permanence of things that preceded
you and held you when no one else would?

What endures has no memory—
oyster shells still bleaching, cannon balls
with no blood or bone attached,
tabby walls where a church once stood.

Grocery Shopping

On Saturday mornings I bought groceries
while my father went to the drugstore
and the dry cleaners. At home my mother
rarely ate. Emaciated and bedridden
at 33 her face looked 50.

From her sick bed, my little brother and I
must have seemed like frenetic birds.
Swooping in and out of her room
with report cards, torn jackets, or the day's mail.
We did anything to distract her.

And my father, always the Marine
in charge, suddenly turned househusband,
sustained by monthly transfusions,
was preoccupied and quiet.
His clear skin whitening like ice.

In our house, where time was hiding
in a box we never found, it seemed
my parents were not running
toward or away from death, but reluctantly
turning their heads in its direction.

Grief, the Color of Dahlias

On my mother's first grim anniversary
I walked through rows of flower stalls
in the outdoor market in Cuernevaca,

grabbing every color I could find spilling over
the tops of knee-high white plastic buckets,
until my arms were filled with blossoms

for my young widowed mother.
The chatter of the women selling flowers
hovered in the August heat like birdsong.

I didn't understand a word, but I saw
how they hid their grief beneath layers
of cloth the color of dahlias. Each day

started in sun light and ended
with thick rain. It was the season.
That evening, my mother screamed

in the kitchen, when she saw the goat's skull
floating in the soup pot on top of the stove.
It was louder than thunder crashing

down the mountains outside the city,
the ones still covered in snow and the crumbling
remains of pyramids built by an Aztec King.

Pine Pitch

For my Uncle, Jerry Smith

Clustered around the edges
of my father's open grave,
the grown-ups lean into one
another like bunches of crows,
pressing their pale wet faces
against the emptiness
of the slate sky gathering
in the late winter wind.
The flapping minister's robes
sound like sails unfurling
beside the coffin. It is
as if this man carries
the sea inside of him,
the way my father did.

Pine boughs cover the coffin.
Arranged like flowers from one
end to the other, they fill
the air with Christmas smells.
I think of my uncle, climbing
at dusk through falling snow
to do the one thing he could
still do for this man he loved
like a brother. I consider
the tenderness and courage
it must have taken to tear
the branches one by one,
from the mountainside. And how,
when his arms were full of pine,
he ran stumbling down
the trail he had made alone
through the woods. His hands covered
in dark patches of pitch
that stayed on his skin for days.

While It Snows

For my brother, Jack Heath

While it snows you sleep hard
in a rented hospital bed
now dominating the den.
The vac pump cleaning your wound
gurgles and sings. While it snows
a neighbor shovels a path
to the front door. Cars pass
with Christmas trees tied to roofs.
It is Sunday. Twice you saw God—
twice torn from that light
that bathed you and felt like snow
falling at once inside
and outside your body.
While you sleep it snows hard
And I sit beside you
watching you breathe.

As the Tulips Yawn and Crack Open and Fall Apart

In Memory of Mary Anne Smith

she finds feathers   the color and curve
of cut fingernails   tangled
in winter   twigs and the memory
of snow   a nest she will keep

like a secret   this unexpected   blooming
such small white petaled spiral
starflowers   weaving underfoot
despite daffodils   neglected

spring   chickweed   everywhere
love's echo   if only she   had
known how   to bend
down   and smell this happiness

Illuminata

For Jodi Novak

Day One

On the first day of chemo
unexplained gifts appear on the doormat—
lavender soap wrapped in tissue paper,
a thick bar of dark chocolate and a quartz
sparkled rock to keep you earthbound.

Day Two

The saints must be busy today.
That's okay. You watch patterns of sun-
light slide across your bedroom wall.
The dog sleeps on top of your bed
and watches you carefully.

Day Three

Dried leaves in a pile woven together
by spider webs on the brick steps
have no meaning. But they hold
your attention for too long.   Sleep now,
and wait for something green to appear.

Day Four

Late last night, your sister phoned.
You don't ask what took her so long,
because her voice is the one that answers
in dreams. It is the flame
singing through the longest night.

Day Five

Sunflowers tied with yellow velvet ribbon
greet you when you open the front door.
Peaches in a brown bag, a box of pastries
tied with a string, and bowl full of tomatoes.
The note is from a neighbor you hardly know.

Day Six

New copies of *People* and *Vogue* stacked
beneath a bottle of bright pink nail polish
the sticky note attached—"Something to do!"
"2 DVD's that will make you LAUGH—
Pink Panther and *A Fish Called Wanda.*"

Day Seven

After smoking the joint that was hidden
in an envelope labeled JUST IN CASE,
you look up the word *grace* in the dictionary.
"Thank you for the gifts," you write,
"I feel like a saint has visited my doorstep."

Surrounded by Flowers, Floating in Light

In Memory of Margaret Kays

At breakfast we speak of cancer.
How the very thing that cures
can kill you, and sometimes does.

Everyone has a story—
The neighbor with a brain tumor
who died of leukemia

caused by chemotherapy,
or the one about the staph
infection post-surgery,

the grandfather who caught
pneumonia during his last
hospital stay. All the while,

a tiny orange and blue
butterfly clings to the white
wall of the dining room, wings

beating bravely. The hidden
source of its own resilience,
as mysterious as light.

Or air, that holds each last breath
taken, on beds where the dying
have lain for days, hovering

at the edges of their lives
until the light enters them.
Until that is all there is,

and we can only watch them
fade slowly. Late evening
after visiting hours

the hospital hums to itself.
I visit the darkened rooms,
throbbing with machinery.

On the oncology floor
the doors are shut. Behind them,
is a kind of loneliness

that can't be shared. I enter,
carrying flowers—sweet and
blooming, which is how I want

to remember her. Propped-up
with white pillows, her eyes wide
and radiant, but empty

of flame, Margaret has tossed
the bright baseball caps and scarves.
Whatever hope she'd held, now

dissolving into lost hours.
Her outline already melting
like a shadow on the sheets.

Gasping after each word
spoken above the soft swish
of monitors and pumps,

she says her young son's visits
exhaust her. She sleeps all day
to prepare herself for him.

The card we made stretches
like a chain cross two walls.
She's never taking it down,

nor the picture of yellow
flowers she painted last week,
sitting up in her wheelchair

for almost an hour, her
son on her lap with his own
paper and paints making

a little house just for him
and his mom. It is painted
blue, the color of the sky.

The sun blazing in the top
left corner fills half the paper
with thick yellow streaks that stop

just above the little house
with white trim, surrounded by
gardens, floating in light.

Behind the Pines

In memory of Edward Murray

Two blocks from the port terminal
as docked ships unload containers
of sand colored tanks, Chinese sneakers,
and Egyptian spoons; at the stoplight
where the off-ramp splits into three lanes,
spilling cars into civilization,

people pause on the way home, shedding
hours of the day in this still space
that is only theirs. They listen for news
of the world, songs spinning in their heads.
In their hearts is what waits and the longing
for what is not found there. And this

is the moment they allow for that
small reckoning with themselves,
the way a song will seem to be sung
just for them. And then it passes.
They look up, out the window
at rows of pine trees which amaze

with their height and that dark green
which must be the color of life itself,
because of the way these trees thrive
beside miles of concrete and a river
that has disappeared. Away from the shops
and the long labyrinth of neighborhoods

hidden from the highway,
behind a small forest of pines
is a house where people come to die—
where the sounds of the world are muted
and each small room holds one bed, one chair,
and a painting of a single boat at sea.

Nothing Can Contain You

In memory of David Hilderbrand

Not the wreath woven from fresh flowers,
nor the photograph it rings. Not the calm
smile at the center. Not the messages
inscribed by the ones who loved you most.
Not your initials, nor the dates
marked in black lettering across the white
cross, planted behind the guard rail
at the edge of a Georgia highway—
the one perpetually filling with sunlight.

But birds….there should be birds.
Small and many. Birds that have just come
from the sea, which can't be far. There should be
one for each year. They should descend in a rush
and surprise, and smother the small trees
growing in a line beyond the roadside
memorial. They should be white. And from
a distance, it would look like a line of crosses
trembling beneath a violet sky, full of song.

Seeking

For Jonathan Green

It happens in   stillness. Because it is night
you hear snakes drop   from the oak
and other things   you can not name
passing   beneath or above you. Trees
so thick the stars are   mute.
Close   your eyes. The immensity
of such unquantifiable   light
fills   the emptiness   that once was
memory. After   the hunger
and solitude, dreams   and the dead
speaking   as if they are   with you,
it happens   when the oak   begins to burn
from within. And   you   welcome the flames.

Notes

"The Endless Repetition of an Ordinary Miracle" from *Snow* by Orhan Pamuk.

"Annunciation" was commissioned for a project at The Indianapolis Museum of Art. The painting is a *Triptych of the Annunciation, Master of the Legend of St. Ursula.* It is dedicated to my friend, poet and editor Harriet Popham Rigney, whose faith gives me strength.

In "Geography of Home" the phrase "let us be happy when we are happy" from Ingmar Bergman's film *Fanny and Alexander.*

"All Things are Palpable, None are Known" is from John Ashbery's poem "Poem in Three Parts" from his book *Self-Portrait in a Convex Mirror.*

"Elysium, Islands of the Blessed": "In a building built on sand/ beneath a blurry dome/ of heaven" refers to *Every Human Being Stands Beneath His Own Dome of Heaven (Jeder Mensch steht unter seiner Himmelskugel)* Ansolm Keifer's painting of 1970.

"Schlindlerjuden" is the term used for the Jews that were saved from the Nazis by Oskar Schindler. This poem is inspired by the last scene of the Steven Spielberg film *Schindler's List.*

"This is a Day with Ghosts in it." from the poem "Winter Mix" in the book *Pslam* by Carol Ann Davis, published by Tupelo Press.

In "Kambujan Eulogy" Kambujan is the Sanskrit word for Cambodia.

"In Gaza's Berry Fields" based on Steven Erlnager's article "In Gaza's Berry Fields, a Family Reels After Losing 7 Boys to Israeli Fire" from *The New York Times*, January 7, 2005.

"What Remains"—the killing fields refers to the sites where Cambodians were killed and buried by the Khmer Rouge regime, during the genocide between 1975 to 1979. In Hmong culture, a string is tied to a newborn's wrist on the third morning after birth in a soul-calling ceremony. The white string insures that the baby's soul will stay in the body.

"Perhaps an Angel Looks Like Everything We Have Forgotten" is from John Ashberry's poem "Self-Portrait in a Convex Mirror," from his book *Self-Portrait in A Convex Mirror.*

"As the Tulips Yawn and Crack Open and Fall Apart" is from John Ashbery's poem "Grand Galop" from his book *Self-Portrait in a Convex Mirror.* The poem is dedicated to Mary Anne Smith, who took her life in 2009.

"While It Snows" is dedicated to my brother Jack Heath who was recovering from life threatening surgery at Christmastime 2009.

"Illuminata" is inspired by stories that my students in the Expressions of Healing Program at Roper St. Francis Hospital have told me over the years. It is dedicated to my friend Jody Novak, who is a cancer survivor.

"Surrounded By Flowers, Floating in Light" is dedicated to the memory of Margaret Kays, who was a cancer patient and student in the Expressions of Healing Program I teach at Roper St. Francis Hospital.

"Behind the Pines" is dedicated to Edward Murray who died at the Hospice Center located in Mt. Pleasant, South Carolina, which is described in this poem.

"Nothing Can Contain You" was commissioned by Ken Daniels for his film *David's Cross*. The poem is inspired by the roadside memorial for David Hilderbrand, who was killed in a car accident as a teenager near Savannah, Georgia.

"Seeking" was created for a multi-arts celebration of Lowcountry art and culture inspired by a painting by Jonathan Green entitled "Seeking." *SEEKING, Poetry and Prose Written in Response to Jonathan Green's Painting*, edited by Kwame Dawes and Marjory Wentworth, is forthcoming from USC Press.

MARJORY HEATH WENTWORTH is Poet Laureate of South Carolina, and her poems have appeared in numerous books and magazines. Her books of poetry include *Noticing Eden, Despite Gravity,* and *What the Water Gives Me,* a collaboration with artist Mary Edna Fraser. Her children's story, *Shackles,* recently won a Silver Moonbeam Award, and she has been nominated for The Pushcart Prize four times. Marjory teaches poetry in "Expressions of Healing," at Roper St. Francis Cancer Center. She also teaches in a poets-in-the-schools program at Burke High School in Charleston, SC.

Marjory serves on the Board of Directors for the Lowcountry Initiative for the Literary Arts (LILA), The Poetry Society of SC, the University of SC Poetry Initiative, and the Yo Art Project. Her work is included in the South Carolina Poetry Archives at Furman University. Ms. Wentworth also works as a book publicist.

MARY EDNA FRASER uses aerial landscape photographs as the foundation for her artwork, often taken from the family's vintage 1946 Ercoupe plane. Her pioneering contemporary monotypes and large-scale batiks (an ancient process using wax and dyes on cloth) have been collected and exhibited worldwide. Duke University Museum of Art, Gibbes Museum of Art, the National Academy of Sciences, the National Science Foundation, and the Smithsonian National Air and Space Museum have featured her collaborations with scientist Orrin Pilkey as well as with Marjory Wentworth. Interpreting the beauty and change of the planet is a recurring theme in her artwork, which she hopes will act as a catalyst for preservation.

Mary Edna resides in Charleston, SC with her husband John Sperry. See more of her artwork at www.maryedna.com.